Holiday Treats Cookbook

Edited by Megan E. Bryant
Designed by Victoria M. Hammer

GROSSET & DUNLAP
Published by the Penguin Group
Penguin Group (USA) Inc., 375 Hudson Street, New York, New York 10014, U.S.A.
Penguin Group (Canada), 90 Eglinton Avenue East, Suite 700, Toronto, Ontario, Canada M4P 2Y3
(a division of Pearson Penguin Canada Inc.)
Penguin Books Ltd, 80 Strand, London WC2R ORL, England
Penguin Ireland, 25 St Stephen's Green, Dublin 2, Ireland
(a division of Penguin Books Ltd)
Penguin Group (Australia), 250 Camberwell Road, Camberwell, Victoria 3124, Australia
(a division of Pearson Australia Group Pty Ltd)
Penguin Books India Pvt Ltd, 11 Community Centre, Panchsheel Park, New Delhi - 110 017, India
Penguin Group (NZ), Cnr Airborne and Rosedale Roads, Albany, Auckland 1310, New Zealand
(a division of Pearson New Zealand Ltd)
Penguin Books (South Africa) (Pty) Ltd, 24 Sturdee Avenue, Rosebank, Johannesburg 2196, South Africa
Penguin Books Ltd, Registered Offices:
80 Strand, London WC2R ORL, England

Holiday Treats Cookbook

By Ann Bryant
Illustrated by Lisa Workman

Grosset & Dunlap

Hello! I'm Strawberry Shortcake, and I'm berry excited—the holidays are almost here! The holiday season is berry special—it's a time to give thanks for the people you love and remind them how much they mean to you. One of my favorite ways to do that is by making yummy treats for everyone to enjoy. My friends feel the same way, so we decided to put all of our favorite holiday recipes in one book. Now we can make them whenever we want!

This book has lots of delicious recipes to help you celebrate the holidays. Before you start cooking, make sure you read the list of kitchen rules on the next page. And you should <u>always</u> have an adult in the kitchen to help.

HAPPY HOLIDAYS—
　　　　and happy cooking!

　Love,
　　　Strawberry Shortcake

Berry Important Kitchen Rules

- Always ask an adult for permission to use the kitchen. Better yet, ask an adult to help!

- Before you begin, read the entire recipe (from start to finish!) and make sure you have all of the ingredients and supplies you'll need.

- Wash your hands well with soap and water.

- Measure the ingredients carefully. (There are measuring tips on page 14 that will help you measure just the right amount.)

- Follow each step of the recipe exactly as directed.

- Wash all fruits and vegetables.

- Some raw foods—like meat, chicken, fish, and eggs— can have germs in them that can cause food poisoning. It's berry important to cook these foods completely. Always wash your hands well after handling raw meat or eggs. Use separate cutting boards and utensils for raw meats and vegetables.

- Keep cold foods cold and hot foods hot—this helps food stay fresh and keeps germs from growing. Cover and store leftover food in the refrigerator or freezer.

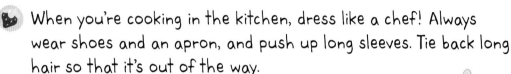

- Always have an adult in the kitchen to help when working at the stove, cutting with knives, handling sharp kitchen tools, and using electrical appliances.

- When you're cooking in the kitchen, dress like a chef! Always wear shoes and an apron, and push up long sleeves. Tie back long hair so that it's out of the way.

- Always use pot holders when handling hot items from the microwave, stove, or oven.

- Turn the handles of skillets and saucepans away from you so that you don't accidentally knock them over. Make sure that the handles are not over a burner—that will make them very hot.

- Clean up as you go—it's safer and easier that way.

- Wash cookie cutters thoroughly in warm water and soap before and after each use.

TIP

When you see this symbol in a recipe, it means that an adult should do that step.

In the Kitchen

Here are some tools you may use when you cook:

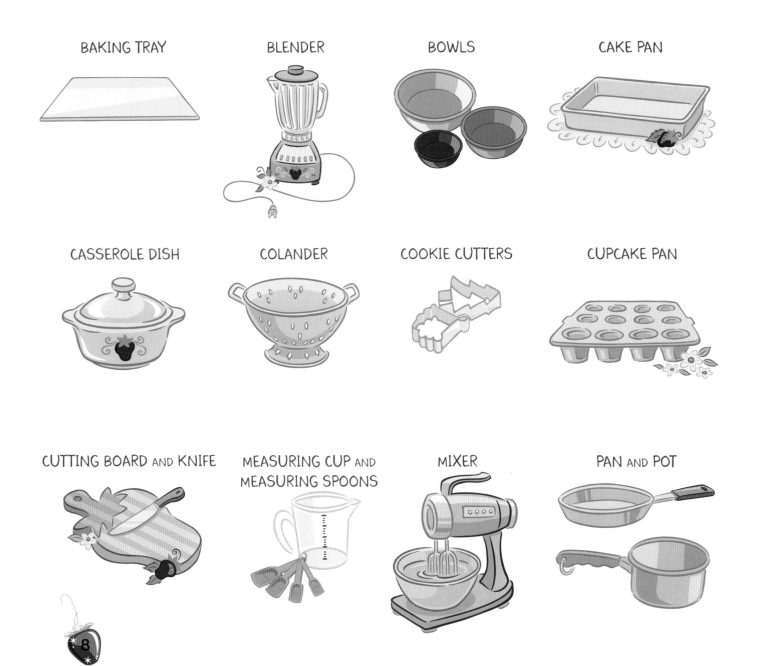

BAKING TRAY

BLENDER

BOWLS

CAKE PAN

CASSEROLE DISH

COLANDER

COOKIE CUTTERS

CUPCAKE PAN

CUTTING BOARD AND KNIFE

MEASURING CUP AND MEASURING SPOONS

MIXER

PAN AND POT

8

ROLLING PIN

SIFTER

SPATULAS

WHISK

WIRE RACK

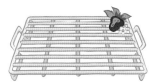

WOODEN SPOON

Look for the Strawberry Key on each recipe . . .

One strawberry means that the recipe is easy—
you can do most of the steps yourself.

Two strawberries mean that the recipe is a little harder—
there are some steps that an adult needs to do.

Three strawberries mean that the recipe is challenging,
so you and an adult can do it together!

Of course,
even if a recipe is easy,
it's important to have an
adult in the kitchen
whenever you cook.

Cooking Terms

<u>BAKE:</u> To cook something in a hot oven

<u>BEAT:</u> To stir ingredients quickly until they are combined

<u>BLEND:</u> To gently mix ingredients together, or to mix ingredients in a blender

<u>BOIL:</u> To cook something in an extremely hot liquid (usually water)—you can tell when a liquid is boiling when steam rises from it and there are lots of little bubbles in it

 <u>CHOP:</u> To cut an ingredient into even-sized pieces

<u>COMBINE:</u> To mix ingredients together

<u>CORE:</u> To remove the seeds and stem from an apple

<u>CREAM:</u> To mix ingredients together until they are smooth (this term usually refers to mixing butter and sugar together when baking)

CRIMP: To seal together two pieces of dough by using your fingers or a fork to pinch or press them together

DICE: To cut an ingredient into very small squares

DRAIN: To pour food into a strainer or colander to remove liquid from it

FOLD: To add an ingredient by gently covering it with a mixture without stirring or beating.

FROST: To decorate a cake or cupcakes with frosting

FRY: To cook a food in a pan using oil or butter

GRATE: To cut foods into tiny bits or slices (you will need a grater or food processor to do this)

GREASE: To smear a pan with butter or oil so that food doesn't stick to it

ICE: To decorate cookies with icing

KNEAD: To press and squeeze dough with your hands until the ingredients are fully combined and the dough is ready for the next step of the recipe

LEVEL: To evenly measure dry ingredients (use a flat knife to brush off any extra)

MINCE: To cut food into tiny pieces

MIX: To combine ingredients by stirring them together

PEEL: To remove the skin from a fruit or vegetable

PINCH: A very small amount (usually salt, pepper, or spices)—use your thumb and forefinger to measure a "pinch"

PREHEAT: To heat the oven to the right temperature before using it

PURÉE: To blend ingredients until completely smooth (you can use a blender or food processor to do this)

ROLL: To use a rolling pin to flatten dough on a smooth surface (sprinkle a small amount of flour on the surface first to keep the dough from sticking)

<u>SHRED:</u> To cut food into small, even strips (you will need a grater or food processor to do this)

<u>SIFT:</u> To remove lumps from a dry ingredient (usually flour) using a sifter or strainer

<u>SLICE:</u> To cut food into equal pieces

<u>STIR:</u> To combine ingredients by mixing them together

<u>TO TASTE:</u> To add an ingredient in very small amounts until it tastes good to you (usually salt, pepper, sugar, or a spice)

<u>WHIP:</u> To beat a liquid ingredient very quickly (using an electric mixer or wire whisk)

<u>WHISK:</u> To beat a liquid ingredient quickly until it breaks up (using an electric mixer, wire whisk, or fork)

TIP
Whenever these words are used in a recipe, they are <u>underlined</u> so that you can come back to this page to look them up if you need to!

Measuring Tips

There are some special rules for measuring these ingredients to make sure you end up with just the right amount.

FLOUR: Gently spoon the flour into the measuring cup. Never use the measuring cup to scoop flour, and don't pack it down with a spoon. Use a butter knife to <u>level</u> off the flour so that you have an even amount.

WHITE SUGAR: Pour or spoon white sugar into the measuring cup. Use a butter knife to <u>level</u> it off.

BROWN SUGAR: Spoon brown sugar into the measuring cup, using the spoon to firmly pack it down as you go.

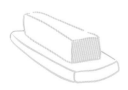

<u>BUTTER:</u> If you buy butter in sticks, the wrapper has printed lines to help you measure it. One stick of butter equals ½ cup.

Table of Contents

Cookies

Huckleberry Pie's
Festive Fudge

Huck makes the best fudge in Strawberryland! During the holidays, he adds colored mini marshmallows to make the fudge extra-yummy.

INGREDIENTS
$\frac{1}{2}$ cup butter
2 cups semisweet chocolate chips
1 teaspoon vanilla
$1\frac{1}{4}$ cup graham cracker crumbs
2 cups colored mini marshmallows

SUPPLIES
Small saucepan
Measuring cups and spoons
Wooden spoon
Large bowl
Waxed paper
Cutting board and knife

TIP

You can buy graham cracker crumbs ready-made or make them yourself by crushing whole graham crackers in a food processor. If you don't have them, don't worry! The fudge is just as yummy on its own.

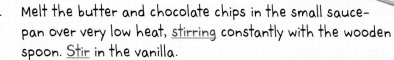

1. Melt the butter and chocolate chips in the small sauce-pan over very low heat, <u>stirring</u> constantly with the wooden spoon. <u>Stir</u> in the vanilla.

2. When the butter and chocolate chips are completely melted and combined, pour the mixture into the bowl and let cool for 10–15 minutes, until slightly warm but still liquid.

3. While the chocolate mixture is cooling, tear five 8-inch-long pieces of waxed paper and sprinkle each with $\frac{1}{4}$ cup graham cracker crumbs.

4. <u>Stir</u> the marshmallows into the chocolate mixture.

5. Divide the fudge into five sections and place each one on a piece of waxed paper. <u>Roll</u> the fudge in the waxed paper so that it is covered by the graham cracker crumbs. Refrigerate for at least 4 hours, or until the fudge is firm.

6. Unwrap the fudge from the waxed paper and cut it into $\frac{1}{2}$-inch slices.

Cookies

Ginger Snap's
Candy Cane Cookies

Ginger Snap taught me how to make these yummy peppermint cookies—they're as much fun to make as they are to eat!

INGREDIENTS

$3\frac{1}{2}$ cups flour

1 teaspoon baking powder

$\frac{1}{8}$ teaspoon salt

2 sticks butter, softened

1 cup white sugar

1 egg

$\frac{1}{2}$ cup milk

$1\frac{1}{2}$ teaspoons vanilla

$\frac{1}{2}$ teaspoon peppermint extract

red food coloring

2 tablespoons crushed peppermint candies

2 tablespoons white sugar

SUPPLIES

Baking tray and wire rack

2 bowls (medium and large)

Measuring cups and spoons

Dish towel

Foil

Spatula and wooden spoon

Electric mixer

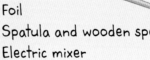

20

1. <u>Preheat</u> the oven to 375 degrees.

2. Line a baking tray with foil.

 3. In the medium bowl, <u>stir</u> together the flour, baking powder, and salt.

4. In the large bowl, <u>cream</u> together the butter and sugar using the electric mixer. Add the egg and <u>beat</u> until combined. Then <u>mix</u> in the milk, vanilla, and peppermint extract.

5. Slowly pour the flour mixture into the butter mixture, with the beaters on low. <u>Mix</u> until well-combined.

6. Divide the dough in half; set aside one half and cover it with a dish towel to keep it moist.

7. Add red food coloring to half of the dough, and <u>knead</u> until the dough is an even shade of red without any streaks of food coloring remaining.

8. <u>Roll</u> 1 teaspoon of red dough into a 4-inch rope. Repeat with 1 teaspoon of white dough. Lay the two ropes of dough next to each other, then twist them together. Curve one end over so that it looks like a candy cane. Repeat for each cookie.

 9. Place the cookies on the baking tray (make sure they are evenly spaced) and <u>bake</u> for 10–12 minutes, or until the cookies are done. Use the spatula to carefully remove the cookies from the tray and let cool on a wire rack.

TIP

For extra-special candy cane cookies, <u>mix</u> together 2 tablespoons crushed peppermint candies and 2 tablespoons white sugar, and sprinkle the mixture onto the cookies as soon as they come out of the oven.

Sugar Cookies for Santa

I love making sugar cookies! They're berry fun to decorate with all kinds of icings and toppings. I think Santa likes my sugar cookies, too— there are never any left on the plate I leave for him!

INGREDIENTS
$3\frac{1}{4}$ cups flour
$\frac{1}{2}$ teaspoon baking soda
$\frac{1}{4}$ teaspoon salt
1 cup butter, softened
$1\frac{1}{4}$ cup white sugar
2 eggs
1 tablespoon vanilla extract
1 batch cookie icing (recipe on page 23)

SUPPLIES
2 bowls (medium and large)
Measuring cups and spoons
Electric mixer
Plastic wrap
Baking tray
Foil
Rolling pin
Cookie cutters
Spatula
Wire rack

1. In the medium bowl, <u>combine</u> the flour, baking soda, and salt.

2. In the large bowl, <u>cream</u> together the butter and sugar using the electric mixer. Add the egg, and <u>mix</u> until well-combined. Then <u>mix</u> in the vanilla.

3. Slowly add the flour mixture to the butter mixture, and <u>beat</u> on medium speed until the ingredients are fully combined.

4. Cover the bowl with plastic wrap and refrigerate for 1 to 2 hours, until the dough is cold and firm.

5. <u>Preheat</u> the oven to 350 degrees, and line a baking tray with foil.

6. Sprinkle a clean, flat surface with a tablespoon of flour, and use the rolling pin to <u>roll</u> out half of the dough. The dough should be about $\frac{1}{8}$ inch thick.

7. Now use cookie cutters to cut out all sorts of fun shapes! Place the shapes on the baking tray.

8. <u>Bake</u> the cookies for 5–7 minutes, or until light golden brown. Use the spatula to transfer the cookies to a wire rack so they can cool.

9. While one batch of cookies is baking, repeat steps 6 and 7 until all of the cookies are baked.

10. After the cookies have cooled, you can decorate them any way you want!

TIP
If you don't have time to <u>ice</u> the cookies, sprinkle colored sugar on them before baking. They will look just as pretty!

Cookie Icing

Sugar cookies taste great all by themselves—but you can have a berry fun time decorating them with pretty icing!

INGREDIENTS

4 tablespoons butter, softened
2 cups powdered sugar
4 tablespoons milk
1 teaspoon vanilla
Food coloring
Sprinkles or small candies

SUPPLIES

Bowls (1 medium for mixing the icing, 1 small bowl for each color you want to make)
Measuring cups and spoons
Electric mixer
Fork
Butter knife or small spatula

TIP

You can easily make a pastry bag to add tiny amounts of icing as decoration to your cookies. Cut off a small corner of a plastic zippered bag, then spoon icing into it and seal the bag. When you press on the bag, icing will squeeze out of the corner and you can control where it goes.

1. <u>Combine</u> the butter, sugar, milk, and vanilla in the medium bowl and <u>beat</u> with the electric mixer until completely smooth.

2. Separate the icing into multiple small bowls, one for each color. Add a few drops of food coloring to each bowl and <u>mix</u> with a fork until the icing is all one color, without streaks of food coloring. If you want brighter colors, add more food coloring.

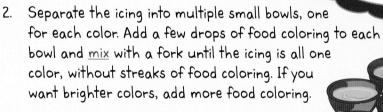

3. Spread the icing onto cooled cookies with a butter knife or small spatula.

4. You can also add small candies or sprinkles to decorate your cookies. Be creative and have fun!

Angel Cake's
Present Cookies

Biting into one of these cookies is just like opening a present—you never know what nice surprise will be inside!

INGREDIENTS

2 cups flour

$\frac{1}{2}$ teaspoon baking soda

$\frac{1}{4}$ teaspoon salt

1 cup butter, softened

1 cup white sugar

1 egg

1 tablespoon vanilla

One or more of the following fillings: jam, peanut butter, chocolate chips, marshmallow fluff, raisins, or dried fruit

Colored sugar (optional)

SUPPLIES

2 bowls (medium and large)

Measuring cups and spoons

Electric mixer

Plastic wrap

Baking tray

Foil

Rolling pin

Butter knife and fork

Spatula

Wire rack

24

1. In the medium bowl, <u>combine</u> the flour, baking soda, and salt.

2. Use the electric mixer to <u>cream</u> together the butter and the sugar in the large bowl. Add the egg and vanilla and <u>beat</u> until fluffy.

3. Slowly add the flour mixture to the butter mixture, and <u>beat</u> until all the ingredients are combined.

4. Cover the bowl with plastic wrap and refrigerate the dough for at least 2 hours, or until it is cold and firm.

5. <u>Preheat</u> the oven to 350 degrees.

6. Line a baking tray with foil.

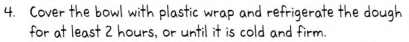
7. Sprinkle a clean, flat surface with a tablespoon of flour, and use the rolling pin to <u>roll</u> out half of the dough. The dough should be about $\frac{1}{8}$ inch thick.

8. Use the butter knife to cut the dough into 2x2-inch squares. Place the squares on the baking tray about 1 inch apart.

9. Place 1 teaspoon of filling in the center of each square. Then top with another square. Use the tines of a fork to <u>crimp</u> the edges closed. If you want, sprinkle each present cookie with colored sugar to make it look like a wrapped present.

10. <u>Bake</u> for 10–15 minutes, or until the cookies are done. Use the spatula to carefully transfer the cookies to the wire rack so they can cool.

TIP

If you want, use decorator icing to make "bows" on the present cookies.

Strawberry Shortcake's
Jam Dot Cookies

I just love strawberry jam! Cookies with jam in them are one of my berry favorite treats.

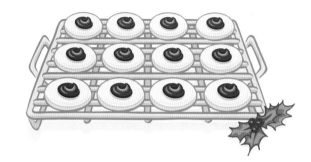

INGREDIENTS
$2\frac{1}{2}$ cups flour

$1\frac{1}{2}$ teaspoons baking soda

$\frac{1}{4}$ teaspoon salt

1 cup butter, softened

$1\frac{1}{2}$ cups white sugar

1 egg

1 tablespoon vanilla extract

$\frac{1}{2}$ cup strawberry jam

SUPPLIES
Baking tray

Foil

2 bowls (medium and large)

Measuring cups and spoons

Electric mixer

Small glass bowl

Spoon

Spatula

Wire rack

1. <u>Preheat</u> the oven to 350 degrees.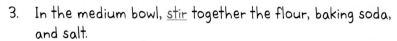

2. Line a baking tray with foil.

 3. In the medium bowl, <u>stir</u> together the flour, baking soda, and salt.

 4. In the large bowl, <u>cream</u> together the butter and the sugar using the electric mixer. Then <u>mix</u> in the egg and vanilla.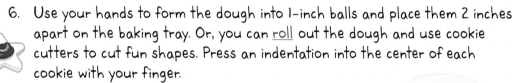

 5. Add the flour mixture to the butter mixture and <u>beat</u> on medium speed until all the ingredients are combined.

6. Use your hands to form the dough into 1-inch balls and place them 2 inches apart on the baking tray. Or, you can <u>roll</u> out the dough and use cookie cutters to cut fun shapes. Press an indentation into the center of each cookie with your finger.

7. Melt the jam in the small glass bowl in the microwave on medium power.

8. Spoon a small amount of jam into each cookie, then <u>bake</u> for 10–15 minutes, or until the cookies are done. Carefully move the cookies to the wire rack so they can cool.

TIP

Melted jam can be berry hot, so be extra-careful!

Raspberry Torte's
Chocolate-Raspberry Rugelach

Mmm, I love this cookie! A rugelach is a rolled-up cookie made of flaky dough with lots of yummy flavors inside.

INGREDIENTS

6 ounces cream cheese, softened and cut into quarters

1 cup butter, softened

2¾ cups flour

½ cup white sugar

1 teaspoon cinnamon

1 egg

1 tablespoon cold water

1 cup seedless raspberry jam

1 cup mini chocolate chips

SUPPLIES

4 bowls

Measuring cups and spoons

Plastic wrap

Baking tray

Foil

Rolling pin

Knife

Spatula

Wire rack

TIP

It's easier to work with the dough when it's nice and cold, so take only one piece out of the refrigerator at a time.

1. Use the electric mixer to <u>combine</u> the cream cheese and butter. Add the flour and <u>beat</u> until fully combined.

2. Divide the dough into four pieces and wrap them tightly in plastic wrap. Refrigerate the dough for 1–2 hours, or until cold and firm.

3. After the dough has chilled, <u>mix</u> 2 tablespoons of the sugar and the cinnamon in a small bowl, and set aside.

4. <u>Preheat</u> the oven to 375 degrees.

5. Line a baking tray with foil.

6. <u>Beat</u> the egg and the water, and set aside.

7. Melt the raspberry jam in the microwave on medium power—be careful; melted jam can be very hot.

8. Sprinkle a clean, flat surface with a tablespoon of flour, and use the rolling pin to <u>roll</u> out one piece of the dough into a 10-inch circle.

9. Spread $\frac{1}{4}$ cup of jam over the dough. Then sprinkle with $\frac{1}{4}$ tablespoon of the cinnamon sugar. Finally, sprinkle $\frac{1}{4}$ cup of the chocolate chips on top.

10. Cut the dough into ten wedge-shaped pieces and, starting at the wide edge, roll up each one.

11. Repeat steps 8–10 for each piece of dough.

12. Place the cookies about 1 inch apart on the baking tray. Brush each cookie with the beaten egg and sprinkle with the remaining white sugar.

13. <u>Bake</u> for 15–20 minutes, or until golden. Let cool on wire racks.

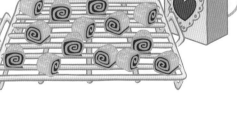

Blueberry Muffin's
Mandelbroit

Mandelbroit is a crunchy cookie that tastes like vanilla. It's nice for dunking into warm, sweet drinks!

INGREDIENTS

3 cups flour
1 teaspoon baking powder
3 eggs
1 cup white sugar
2 teaspoons vanilla
1 cup vegetable oil
1 cup ground almonds

SUPPLIES

Baking tray
Foil
Sifter
2 bowls (medium and large)
Electric mixer
Cutting board and knife

 1. <u>Preheat</u> the oven to 350 degrees.

2. Line a baking tray with foil.

3. <u>Sift</u> the flour and baking powder into the medium bowl and set aside.

 4. In the large bowl, <u>beat</u> the eggs with the electric mixer. Add the sugar and vanilla and continue mixing. Then add the oil, followed by the flour mixture and the ground almonds. <u>Mix</u> until the ingredients are well-combined.

5. Separate the dough into four pieces and shape each one into a log about 2 inches wide. Place the logs of dough onto the baking tray about 2 inches apart.

6. <u>Bake</u> for about 30 minutes, or until golden brown. While the mandelbroit is still warm, have an adult cut each log into 1-inch slices.

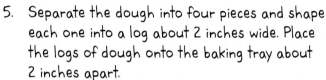

TIP

I like to eat mandelbroit with a warm mug of vanilla milk. There's a recipe for vanilla milk on page 93.

Angel Cake's
Snowball Cookies

These cute little cookies look just like snowballs—
and they're especially nice to eat after playing
in the snow!

INGREDIENTS
$\frac{3}{4}$ cup butter
$\frac{1}{2}$ cup white sugar
$\frac{1}{4}$ teaspoon salt
1 egg
1 teaspoon vanilla
$1\frac{3}{4}$ cups flour
1 cup powdered sugar

SUPPLIES
Baking tray
Foil
Large bowl
Measuring cups and spoons
Electric mixer
Spatula
Wire rack
Sifter
Plastic bag

 1. <u>Preheat</u> the oven to 350 degrees.

2. Line a baking tray with foil.

 3. In the large bowl, <u>cream</u> together the butter and sugar using an electric mixer. Add the salt, egg, and vanilla, <u>mixing</u> constantly. Slowly add the flour and continue <u>mixing</u> until the ingredients are well-combined.

4. When the dough is completely mixed, use your hands to shape it into round, 1-inch balls. Place each ball 2 inches apart on the baking tray.

 5. <u>Bake</u> the cookies for about 15 minutes, or until the bottoms are golden. Let cool for 5 minutes on a wire rack.

6. While the cookies are baking, <u>sift</u> the powdered sugar into a large plastic bag.

7. After the cookies have cooled, place them in the bag full of powdered sugar and gently shake the bag until the cookies are coated with sugar. They will look just like little snowballs! If you want, you can even coat the cookies with powdered sugar twice to make sure they look really snowy.

TIP

Add a yummy surprise to these snowballs by placing a chocolate chip or small candy in the middle of each one during step 4!

Ginger Snap's
Gingerbread People

Ginger Snap and I love making whole families of yummy gingerbread people and decorating them in lots of different ways!

INGREDIENTS

2½ cups flour
1 teaspoon baking soda
2 teaspoons cinnamon
1 teaspoon ground ginger
1 teaspoon nutmeg
¼ teaspoon allspice
1 cup butter, softened
½ cup brown sugar
½ cup molasses
1 egg

1 batch Buttercream Frosting
(recipe on page 59)
Assorted candy for decorating
(you can use peppermints, gumdrops, miniature chocolate candies, jelly beans, candy buttons, sprinkles, miniature marshmallows, or any other small candies you have)

SUPPLIES

2 bowls (medium and large)
Measuring cups and spoons
Wooden spoon
Electric mixer
Plastic wrap

Baking tray
Foil
Rolling pin
Cookie cutters
Spatula
Wire rack

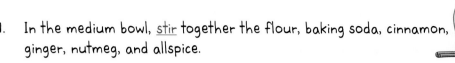

1. In the medium bowl, <u>stir</u> together the flour, baking soda, cinnamon, ginger, nutmeg, and allspice.

2. In the large bowl, <u>cream</u> together the butter and sugar. Then <u>beat</u> in the molasses and egg. Add the flour mixture to the butter mixture and <u>mix</u> until well-combined.

3. Cover the dough with plastic wrap and refrigerate for at least 1 hour, or until cold and firm.

4. <u>Preheat</u> the oven to 350 degrees.

5. Line a baking tray with foil.

6. Sprinkle a clean, flat surface with a tablespoon of flour, and use the rolling pin to <u>roll</u> out half of the dough. The dough should be about $\frac{1}{4}$ inch thick.

7. Use the cookie cutters to cut out your gingerbread people. Place the cookies about $1\frac{1}{2}$ inches apart on the baking tray.

8. <u>Bake</u> for 8–12 minutes, or until cookies are done. Use the spatula to carefully move the cookies to the wire rack so they can cool.

9. When the cookies are cool, use the Buttercream Frosting on page 59 to decorate them! You can add little candies, too.

TIP

For soft and chewy gingerbread cookies, <u>roll</u> the dough 1 inch thick and bake for about 15 minutes.

Strawberry Shortcake's
Holiday Wishes Brownies

Make everybody's holiday wishes come true with these scrumptious brownies! Three different frostings let your family and friends pick their berry favorite flavor.

INGREDIENTS

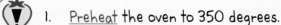

- ½ cup butter
- ¾ cup brown sugar
- ¼ cup cocoa powder
- ½ cup flour
- ½ teaspoon baking powder
- 2 teaspoons vanilla
- 1 batch of frosting (recipes on page 37)

SUPPLIES

Small saucepan
Measuring cups and spoons
Wooden spoon
2 bowls (medium and large)
9x13-inch baking pan
Electric mixer
Toothpick or cake tester
Butter knife or spatula

1. <u>Preheat</u> the oven to 350 degrees.

2. In the small saucepan, melt the butter, brown sugar, and cocoa powder together, <u>stirring</u> constantly until the ingredients are completely combined. Pour the butter mixture into the large bowl and set aside to cool for 15 minutes.

3. While the butter mixture cools, <u>stir</u> together the flour and baking powder in the medium bowl.

4. <u>Grease</u> the baking pan.

5. Slowly add the flour mixture to the butter mixture and <u>beat</u> using the electric mixer until the batter is smooth. <u>Stir</u> in the vanilla.

6. Pour the batter into the baking pan and <u>bake</u> for 30–40 minutes, or until a toothpick or cake tester inserted in the middle of the pan comes out clean (or with crumbs on it).

7. When the brownies are cool, use a butter knife or spatula to <u>frost</u> with the frosting of your choice.

TIP

Cutting brownies with a plastic knife will keep the tops looking neater.

Peanut-Butter Frosting

INGREDIENTS

- 1½ cups powdered sugar
- 2½ tablespoons creamy peanut butter
- 1 teaspoon vanilla
- 2–3 tablespoons milk

Peppermint Frosting

INGREDIENTS

- ¼ cup butter, softened
- 1½ cups powdered sugar
- ¾ teaspoon vanilla
- ¼ teaspoon peppermint extract
- 2–3 tablespoons milk
- Food coloring (optional)

Fudgey Frosting

INGREDIENTS

- ¼ cup butter, softened
- 1½ cups powdered sugar
- 1¾ tablespoons cocoa powder (or more to taste)
- 1 teaspoon vanilla
- 2–3 tablespoons milk

SUPPLIES (for all)

- Small bowl
- Measuring cups and spoons
- Electric mixer

1. <u>Combine</u> all ingredients in the small bowl and <u>beat</u> with an electric mixer until smooth and creamy. If the frosting is too thick, add a little more milk.

TIP

Make the brownies even better by adding chopped peanuts on top of the peanut-butter brownies, crushed peppermint candies on top of the peppermint brownies, or miniature chocolate chips on top of the fudgey brownies!

Orange Blossom's Benne Cakes

Did you know that sesame seeds are also called "benne seeds"? I didn't—until Orange Blossom made these yummy cookies for Kwanzaa and shared them with me! Benne seeds are supposed to bring good luck.

INGREDIENTS

- ½ cup flour
- ½ teaspoon baking powder
- ¼ teaspoon salt
- ¼ cup butter, softened
- 1 cup brown sugar, packed
- 1 egg
- ½ teaspoon vanilla
- 1 teaspoon lemon juice
- 1 cup sesame seeds, toasted

SUPPLIES

- Baking tray
- Foil
- 2 bowls (medium and large)
- Measuring cups and spoons
- Electric mixer
- Spoon
- Spatula
- Wire rack

TIP

To toast the sesame seeds, put them in a small frying pan over medium heat, and cook, stirring constantly, until they are pale golden brown and fragrant.

1. Preheat the oven to 325 degrees and line a baking tray with foil.

2. In the medium bowl, stir together the flour, baking powder, and salt.

3. In the large bowl, cream together the butter and brown sugar with the electric mixer, and beat until fluffy. Add the egg and vanilla and beat until the ingredients are well-combined.

4. Stir in the lemon juice and sesame seeds.

5. Drop rounded tablespoons of dough about 2 inches apart on the baking tray.

6. Bake for 12-15 minutes, or until cookies are done.

38

Ginger Snap's
Snickerdoodles

Ginger Snap loves cookies and spices—so it makes sense that yummy snickerdoodles, with lots of cinnamon sugar, are some of her favorites! And she also likes their funny name!

INGREDIENTS

- 1¾ cups flour
- ½ teaspoon baking soda
- ¼ teaspoon salt
- ½ cup butter, softened
- 1 cup + 2 tablespoons white sugar
- 1 egg
- 2 tablespoons milk or cream
- 2 teaspoons vanilla
- ½ teaspoon cinnamon

SUPPLIES

- Baking tray
- Foil
- 3 bowls (small, medium, large)
- Measuring cups and spoons
- Wooden spoon
- Electric mixer
- Spatula
- Wire rack

TIP

If you have leftover cinnamon sugar, it's better to throw it away than reuse it, since there could be pieces of uncooked cookie dough in it.

1. <u>Preheat</u> the oven to 375 degrees.

2. Line a baking tray with foil.

3. In the medium bowl, <u>stir</u> together the flour, baking soda, and salt. Set aside.

4. Use the electric mixer to <u>cream</u> together the butter and 1 cup of the sugar. (Don't forget to set aside 2 tablespoons of sugar for later!) <u>Beat</u> in the egg. Add the milk and vanilla and <u>beat</u> until all the ingredients are combined.

5. In the small bowl, <u>stir</u> together the 2 tablespoons of sugar and the cinnamon.

6. Use your hands to shape the dough into round, 1-inch balls. Roll the balls in the cinnamon sugar mixture and place them about 2 inches apart on the baking tray.

7. <u>Bake</u> for 10–12 minutes, or until the cookies are done. Use the spatula to carefully move the cookies to the wire rack so they can cool.

Cookie Party

The first snowflakes of the season were fluttering outside the window. "Look, Apple!" I said. "It's snowing!"

"Snow! Snow!" she said happily. "Play in the snow?"

"You got it, sweetie!" I replied. We quickly put on our winter gear and hurried outside.

Just then, Ginger Snap skipped along the Berry Trail. "Hi there, Strawberry and Apple!" she called. "Guess what? I'm having a cookie party today!"

"A cookie party?" I asked. "What's that?"

"You'll see!" Ginger said mysteriously. "Come over to my house at two o'clock, and bring your favorite cookie recipe." She waved and hurried off toward Cakewalk.

"That sounds berry fun!" I said. "See you soon!"

Apple and I paged through all our cookbooks, looking for just the right recipe to bring to Ginger's cookie party.

"Uh-oh!" I said. "It's almost two o'clock now! We'd better hurry or we'll be late!" Apple and I put on our coats and boots again and set off down the Berry Trail to Cookie Corners.

Soon we arrived at Ginger Snap's gingerbread house. Our friends were already there.

"Hi, Strawberry and Apple!" exclaimed Ginger. "What recipe did you bring?"

"Our berry favorite cookie recipe—Jam Dots!" I replied. "Which recipes did everybody else pick?"

"Snowball Cookies for a snowy day," Angel Cake said.

"I brought my favorite fudge recipe," called out Huck.

"Benne Cakes are a nice cookie," Orange Blossom said quietly.

"I picked Snickerdoodles," replied Blueberry Muffin.

"And I'm going to make gingerbread people," Ginger Snap added.

"Wow!" I said. "All of those cookies sound berry delicious! I'd love to try them all."

"Guess what?" asked Ginger. "You can! At a cookie party, everybody makes his or her favorite cookie recipe. Then we share the cookies so that everyone takes home some of each."

"What a great idea, Ginger!" I said happily. "Let's start baking!"

For the next few hours, Ginger Snap's kitchen was filled with yummy cookie smells. By the time the cookie party was over, everybody had a big plate filled with lots of different cookies to share—just in time for the holidays!

Cakes & Pies

Piecrust

You can use this yummy piecrust for any pie you like!
This recipe makes one 9-inch piecrust. If you want a
top crust for your pie, just double the recipe.

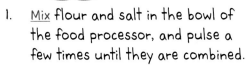

INGREDIENTS

1½ cups flour
¼ teaspoon salt
½ cup butter, chilled
3–4 tablespoons
  ice water

SUPPLIES

Measuring cups and spoons
Food processor (or large bowl
  and pastry blender, or 2 butter
  knives)
Butter knife
Cutting board or
  pastry mat
Plastic wrap
Rolling pin
Spatula
9-inch pie plate

TIP

Always use very cold
butter and icy water when you
make piecrust, and don't
over-<u>mix</u> the ingredients!

1. <u>Mix</u> flour and salt in the bowl of
   the food processor, and pulse a
   few times until they are combined.

2. Cut the butter into 1-inch pieces
   and add to the food processor.
   Pulse 8–10 times, or until the
   dough begins to clump together
   and form pieces the size of small
   peas. (If you don't have a food
   processor, you can use a pastry
   blender or two butter knives to
   <u>mix</u> the butter into the flour.)

3. Drizzle the water into the food
   processor one tablespoon at a
   time, and pulse just until the
   dough forms a ball.

4. Move the dough to a clean, dry
   surface, like a cutting board or
   a pastry mat. Pat the dough into
   a ball and wrap it in plastic wrap.
   Refrigerate for at least 2 hours.

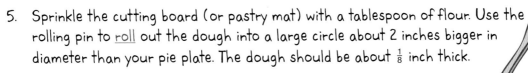

5. Sprinkle the cutting board (or pastry mat) with a tablespoon of flour. Use the rolling pin to <u>roll</u> out the dough into a large circle about 2 inches bigger in diameter than your pie plate. The dough should be about $\frac{1}{8}$ inch thick.

6. Using a spatula, carefully lift the dough and drape it over the pie plate. Use your fingers to lightly press the dough into the plate. Trim any excess dough around the edge of the pie plate.

 7. Continue the recipe according to the directions for adding filling of your choice, and <u>bake</u> as directed.

Whipped Cream

I love whipped cream on pie and cake! Here's an easy recipe for making your berry own whipped cream at home.

INGREDIENTS
2 pints whipping cream
2 tablespoons sugar
2 tablespoons vanilla

SUPPLIES
Medium metal bowl
Measuring cups and spoons
Electric mixer

TIP
Chill the metal bowl and beaters in the freezer for about 30–60 minutes before you make the whipped cream. That helps the cream <u>whip</u> faster.

1. Put the cream, sugar, and vanilla in the bowl.

 2. <u>Mix</u> the ingredients together using the electric mixer on medium speed. The cream will gradually begin to thicken. If you want, add more sugar <u>to taste</u>. When it forms soft peaks, you're done! Be careful not to over-<u>mix</u> it.

Orange Blossom's
Pumpkin Pie

Every fall, Orange Blossom grows the berry best pumpkin patch in the whole wide world! Then she makes yummy pumpkin pies. You don't have to grow your own pumpkin to make this recipe, though—canned pumpkin works just as well.

INGREDIENTS

1 batch of piecrust (recipe on page 44)
1½ cups pumpkin purée
2 eggs
1 cup cream
⅔ cup brown sugar
3 teaspoons vanilla
1 teaspoon cinnamon
¼ teaspoon nutmeg

SUPPLIES

Supplies for making piecrust (see page 44)
Foil
Large bowl
Measuring cups and spoons
Electric mixer
Spatula
Knife
Wire rack

1. Prepare the piecrust according to the recipe on page 44.

 2. <u>Preheat</u> the oven to 450 degrees.

 3. Cover the piecrust with foil and <u>bake</u> for 5 minutes. Remove the foil and <u>bake</u> for 5 more minutes, until crust is barely golden brown. Remove the piecrust from the oven and set aside.

4. In the large bowl, <u>combine</u> the pumpkin purée, eggs, and cream using the electric mixer. <u>Mix</u> until blended. Add the sugar, vanilla, and spices, and <u>beat</u> until the filling is thick and smooth.

 5. Pour the filling into the crust.

 6. <u>Bake</u> for 15 minutes, then turn the heat down to 350 degrees and <u>bake</u> for another 30–40 minutes, or until a knife inserted in the center of the pie comes out clean.

 7. Remove the pie from the oven and cool on a wire rack.

TIP

Pumpkin pie tastes especially good served with whipped cream!

Cakes & Pies

Apple Dumplin's
Apple Pie

My baby sister *loves* apples! This pie is one of her berry favorite holiday treats.

INGREDIENTS

2 batches of piecrust
(recipe on page 44)

6 large (or 8 medium) green apples

$\frac{1}{2}$ cup white sugar

$\frac{1}{2}$ teaspoon cinnamon

$\frac{1}{8}$ teaspoon nutmeg

1 tablespoon flour

1 teaspoon lemon juice

2 tablespoons butter

SUPPLIES

Supplies for making piecrust
(see page 44)

Cutting board and knife

2 bowls (small and large)

Measuring cups and spoons

Spoon

Butter knife

TIP

Make sure you <u>slice</u> the apples into evenly sized pieces so that they cook at the same rate.

1. Double the recipe for piecrust on page 44. Prepare two batches of pie dough through step 4. Split the dough into two equal pieces, wrap with plastic wrap, and refrigerate for at least 2 hours.

2. <u>Preheat</u> the oven to 450 degrees.

3. Wash, <u>peel</u>, and <u>core</u> the apples. Cut them into equal-sized pieces about $\frac{1}{4}$ inch thick. You should have 7–8 cups of sliced apples.

4. In a small bowl, <u>stir</u> together the sugar, cinnamon, nutmeg, and flour. Sprinkle this mixture over the apple slices and <u>stir</u> until coated. Drizzle the lemon juice over the apples and <u>stir</u> until thoroughly mixed.

5. Taste the apples to see if they are sweet enough. If not, sprinkle more sugar over them <u>to taste</u>. You can also add more cinnamon and nutmeg if you want. Set the apple mixture aside.

6. Remove one batch of pie dough from the refrigerator. Sprinkle a clean, flat surface (like a cutting board or pastry mat) with a tablespoon of flour. Use the rolling pin to <u>roll</u> out the dough into a large circle about 2 inches bigger in diameter than your pie pan. The dough should be about $\frac{1}{8}$ inch thick.

7. Carefully lift the dough using a spatula, and drape it over the pie plate. Use your fingers to lightly press the dough into the plate. Trim any excess dough around the edges of the pie plate.

8. Spread the apples in the crust, and evenly dot them with small pieces of butter.

9. Remove the other batch of pie dough from the refrigerator and <u>roll</u> the dough to about $\frac{1}{8}$ inch thick. This is the top crust.

10. Carefully drape the top crust over the apples. Cut any excess dough so that there is only about $\frac{1}{2}$ inch of dough hanging over the edge of the pie plate.

11. <u>Crimp</u> the top crust and bottom crust together so that it has a decorative edge. You can use your fingers to pinch the crusts together, or press the crusts together with the tines of a fork.

 12. Use a sharp knife to cut some evenly spaced slits in the top crust of the pie.

 13. <u>Bake</u> the pie for 30 minutes, then reduce the heat to 350 degrees and <u>bake</u> for an additional 20–30 minutes.

 14. The pie is done when the crust is golden brown and you can easily pierce the apples with a sharp knife. Remove the pie from the oven and let cool on a wire rack.

Huckleberry Pie's
Peppermint Ice-Cream Pie

This yummy ice-cream pie is
a cool holiday treat!

INGREDIENTS

For the crust:
- 1 9-ounce package chocolate wafer cookies
- $\frac{1}{4}$ cup butter

For the filling:
- 6 cups peppermint ice cream, softened
- 2 candy canes
- 1 bag peppermint candies

SUPPLIES

Food processor or rolling pin and waxed paper
Medium-sized microwave-safe bowl
Fork
9-inch pie plate
Spoon
Measuring cups
Wire rack

50

1. <u>Preheat</u> the oven to 350 degrees.

2. Make the crust first. Crush the chocolate wafer cookies in the food processor. If you don't have a food processor, place the cookies between two large sheets of waxed paper and crush them with a rolling pin.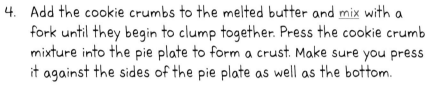

3. Use the microwave to melt the butter in the microwave-safe bowl.

4. Add the cookie crumbs to the melted butter and <u>mix</u> with a fork until they begin to clump together. Press the cookie crumb mixture into the pie plate to form a crust. Make sure you press it against the sides of the pie plate as well as the bottom.

5. <u>Bake</u> the piecrust for 8–10 minutes or until set. Remove from the oven and let cool on a wire rack.

6. When the crust is cool, gently spread the softened ice cream in it. Arrange the two candy canes on top so that they make a heart shape and place the peppermint candies around the outer edge of the pie.

7. Freeze the pie for at least 2 hours, or until the ice cream is frozen solid.

TIP

You can use mint chocolate chip ice cream instead of peppermint to add more chocolate flavor.

Blueberry Muffin's
Blueberry Pound Cake

My friend Blueberry Muffin loves to eat blueberries all year round! In the winter, when she can't grow fresh blueberries, she uses frozen ones in this yummy blueberry pound cake.

INGREDIENTS

3 cups flour

1 teaspoon baking powder

$\frac{1}{2}$ teaspoon salt

1 cup butter, softened

2 cups white sugar

4 eggs

2 teaspoons vanilla

2 cups blueberries (fresh or frozen)

$\frac{1}{4}$ cup powdered sugar (optional)

SUPPLIES

Loaf pan

3 bowls (2 medium, 1 large)

Measuring cups and spoons

Electric mixer

Wooden spoon

Cake tester

Plate

Sifter (optional)

1. <u>Preheat</u> the oven to 325 degrees.

2. <u>Grease</u> and flour a loaf pan.

3. In one of the medium bowls, <u>stir</u> together 2½ cups of the flour with the baking powder and salt. Set aside.

 4. <u>Cream</u> together the butter and sugar in the large bowl, using the electric mixer. Add the eggs one at a time and continue <u>mixing</u> until the batter is fluffy. <u>Mix</u> in the vanilla.

 5. Add the flour mixture to the butter mixture and <u>beat</u> until fully combined.

6. In the other medium bowl, <u>stir</u> together the blueberries and the remaining ½ cup of flour until the blueberries are completely coated with flour.

7. <u>Fold</u> the blueberries into the cake batter with a wooden spoon and gently <u>stir</u> until the blueberries are evenly mixed in.

 8. Pour the batter into the prepared pan and <u>bake</u> for 60–75 minutes, or until a cake tester inserted in the middle comes out clean. Carefully remove the cake from the oven and let cool in the pan for 5–10 minutes before turning onto a plate.

9. Before serving, you can <u>sift</u> powdered sugar on top of the cake to make it look extra-special!

TIP

<u>Mixing</u> the blueberries with the flour keeps their color from staining the batter and also keeps them from sinking to the bottom.

Angel Cake's
Sweetly Spiced Pumpkin Cake

Mmm—this pumpkin cake is full of yummy spices and flavors! Baking it will make your whole house smell good.

INGREDIENTS

2½ cups flour
1½ teaspoons baking soda
1½ teaspoons baking powder
2 teaspoons cinnamon
½ teaspoon nutmeg
½ teaspoon ginger
½ teaspoon ground cloves
¼ teaspoon salt

1 cup oil
2½ cups white sugar
2 cups pumpkin purée
   (or 1 15-ounce can)
3 eggs
2 teaspoons vanilla
1 batch Sweet Glaze
   (recipe on page 55)

TIP
If you don't have a Bundt pan, you can use two round cake pans instead. They will only need to <u>bake</u> for about 30–40 minutes, though.

SUPPLIES

Bundt pan
2 bowls (medium and large)
Measuring cups and spoons
Electric mixer

Cake tester
Wire rack
Supplies for making Sweet Glaze
   (see page 55)

 1. <u>Preheat</u> the oven to 350 degrees, and <u>grease</u> and flour a Bundt pan.

2. In the medium bowl, <u>sift</u> together the flour, baking soda, baking powder, cinnamon, nutmeg, ginger, cloves, and salt. Set aside.

 3. In the large bowl, use the electric mixer to <u>combine</u> the oil and sugar. <u>Beat</u> in the pumpkin. Add the eggs one at a time and <u>mix</u> until well-combined. <u>Stir</u> in the vanilla.

 4. Slowly add the flour mixture to the pumpkin mixture, and <u>beat</u> until all the ingredients are combined and the batter is smooth.

5. Pour the cake batter into the prepared pan.

 6. <u>Bake</u> for 60–75 minutes, or until a cake tester inserted in the cake comes out clean. Let cool in the pan on a wire rack.

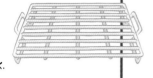

 7. While the cake is cooling, make the Sweet Glaze (recipe on page 55).

8. After the cake is completely cool, remove it from the pan and place it on a pretty plate. Use a spoon to drizzle the Sweet Glaze over the top.

Sweet Glaze

This easy glaze is nice to drizzle over cakes!

INGREDIENTS
- 1 tablespoon butter, softened
- 3 tablespoons milk or cream
- 2 cups powdered sugar

SUPPLIES
- Medium bowl
- Measuring cups and spoons
- Sifter
- Electric mixer

1. Put the butter and milk or cream into the bowl. <u>Sift</u> the powdered sugar into the bowl.

 2. Use the electric mixer to <u>beat</u> together all the ingredients. The glaze should be very thin and smooth, but not runny. If it seems too thick, add another tablespoon or two of milk (or cream).

3. Drizzle over cupcakes or cake.

TIP

<u>Stir</u> in 1 square of melted baking chocolate for chocolate glaze, or $\frac{1}{4}$ cup melted jam for fruit-flavored glaze.

Strawberry Shortcake's
Mini Strawberry Cheesecakes

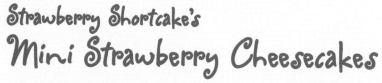

Strawberry cheesecake is one of my berry favorite desserts! These little cheesecakes are perfect for sharing with friends.

INGREDIENTS

For the crust:
- 1 9-ounce package of vanilla wafer cookies or graham crackers
- $\frac{1}{4}$ cup butter

For the filling:
- 2 8-ounce packages of cream cheese
- 1 cup sugar
- 2 eggs
- 2 teaspoons vanilla extract

For the strawberry glaze:
- 1 cup strawberry jam
- 2 teaspoons white sugar
- $\frac{1}{2}$ cup water
- $\frac{1}{2}$ teaspoon cornstarch, dissolved in 1 teaspoon cold water

SUPPLIES

- Muffin tray
- Foil cupcake wrappers
- Food processor (or rolling pin and waxed paper)
- Large bowl
- Measuring cups and spoons
- Saucepan
- Whisk
- Wire rack

1. <u>Preheat</u> the oven to 350 degrees.

2. Line a muffin tray with foil cupcake wrappers.

3. First, make the crust. Crush the wafer cookies or graham crackers in the food processor. If you don't have a food processor, place the cookies between two large sheets of waxed paper and crush them with a rolling pin.

4. Use the microwave to melt the butter in the microwave-safe bowl.

5. Add the cookie crumbs to the melted butter and <u>mix</u> until they clump together. Press about a tablespoon of the cookie crumb mixture into the bottom of each cupcake wrapper to form the crust.

6. <u>Bake</u> the crusts for 5–7 minutes, then remove from the oven and let cool in the muffin tray.

7. Now make the filling. In the large bowl, use the electric mixer to <u>cream</u> together the cream cheese and the sugar until fluffy. Add the eggs, one at a time, followed by the vanilla. <u>Beat</u> until all ingredients are well-combined.

8. Fill each muffin cup $\frac{3}{4}$ of the way with filling.

9. <u>Bake</u> for 5–7 minutes or until set. Remove from the oven and let cool on a wire rack.

10. While the mini cheesecakes are cooling, make the strawberry glaze. Heat the jam, sugar, and water in a small pot and <u>whisk</u> together until fully combined. Slowly add the cornstarch and <u>stir</u> until the glaze is thickened. Let the glaze cool for about 10 minutes.

11. Spoon about a tablespoon of glaze onto each mini cheesecake, and refrigerate until ready to serve.

TIP

You can top the mini cheesecakes with fruit pie filling (cherry is berry nice!) instead of strawberry glaze if you want.

Ginger Snap's
Christmas Tree Cupcakes

These cupcakes are a berry fun treat to make, and they're a perfect dessert for a holiday party! You can use all sorts of yummy candies to decorate them and make them look like real Christmas trees.

TIP

Use chocolate chips for the tree trunk, and make a star at the top of the "tree" out of yellow candies.

INGREDIENTS

1½ cups flour
2 teaspoons baking powder
1 stick butter, softened
½ cup sugar
2 teaspoons vanilla
2 eggs
½ cup milk

1 batch Buttercream Frosting
  (recipe on page 59)
Assorted candies for decorating
  (use peppermints, gumdrops, miniature chocolate candies, jelly beans, candy buttons, miniature marshmallows, or any other small candies you have)
Decorator icing

SUPPLIES

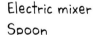

Muffin tray
Foil or paper cupcake wrappers
Measuring cups and spoons
Sifter
2 bowls (small and large)

Electric mixer
Spoon
Wire rack
Supplies for Buttercream
  Frosting (see page 59)

1. <u>Preheat</u> the oven to 350 degrees, and arrange the cupcake wrappers in the muffin tray.

 2. <u>Sift</u> the flour and baking powder into the small bowl.

 3. Use the electric mixer to <u>cream</u> together the butter, sugar, and vanilla. Add the eggs, one at a time, and <u>mix</u> on medium speed until fluffy. Then add the milk and <u>mix</u> until well-combined.

 4. Slowly add the flour mixture to the butter mixture and <u>beat</u> until the batter is smooth.

5. Fill each cupcake wrapper ⅔ of the way.

 6. <u>Bake</u> for 10–15 minutes, or until done. Remove the cupcakes from the oven and cool on a wire rack.

7. While the cupcakes are cooling, prepare the Buttercream Frosting according to the recipe below. Use food coloring to tint the frosting green.

 8. <u>Frost</u> each cupcake, then arrange on a large tray so that the cupcakes make a Christmas-tree shape. Then have fun using the candies and icing to "decorate" the tree!

Buttercream Frosting

This easy frosting tastes great on cake. It's thicker and easier to spread than the Sweet Glaze.

TIP
If the frosting is too thick, add a little more milk. If it's too thin, add more powdered sugar.

INGREDIENTS
POWDERED SUGAR

½ cup butter, softened
1 box powdered sugar
2 teaspoons vanilla
3 tablespoons milk
Food coloring (optional)

SUPPLIES
Medium bowl
Measuring cups and spoons
Electric mixer
Spatula

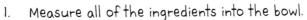

 1. Measure all of the ingredients into the bowl.

2. Use the electric mixer to <u>beat</u> the ingredients together until the frosting is thick and creamy.

Cupcake Surprise

Two weeks before Christmas, I checked my mailbox to find a special invitation from Angel Cake. I called Angel Cake right away. "Hi, Angel! I'd love to come caroling and help you decorate your tree!"

"Great," Angel Cake replied. "See you at the party!"

Angel Cake's invitation reminded me that Apple and I still had to get *our* Christmas tree. So we asked Huckleberry Pie and Ginger Snap to come with us to the Cinnamon Woods to pick one out.

"This is a really nice tree, Strawberry!" Huck said as he helped us load it on our sleigh.

"Thanks!" I said. "And thanks for helping us get it."

"You're welcome," Huck said. "I helped Angel Cake get her tree the other day. It's a really big one!"

"No wonder she wants everybody to come over to help her decorate it," I said.

"I like decorating trees almost as much as I like decorating cookies!" Ginger Snap said. "I can't wait!"

Please come caroling and help decorate the tree!

When: December 20, 6:00

Where: Cakewalk

Why: To get into the holiday spirit!

Please RSVP to Angel Cake

A few days later we all met up at Angel Cake's layer-cake house. She was waiting for us outside with little books filled with the words to holiday songs. We had a berry fun time singing carols through all of Strawberryland until we started to get cold.

"Come on inside, everybody!" Angel Cake said. "I'll make some nice hot drinks and we can start decorating the tree."

But when we got inside, Angel Cake's tree already had lots and lots of ornaments on it.

"Angel Cake, you already decorated your tree!" I said.

"Not *this* tree," replied Angel Cake with a big smile as she came out of her kitchen carrying a platter filled with cupcakes in the shape of a pine tree. "I made a batch of Christmas Tree Cupcakes for us to decorate. I have all kinds of candy in the kitchen so we can make the cupcake tree look like a real Christmas tree."

"What a berry nice holiday surprise!" I said.

"And after we finish decorating the cupcakes, we can eat them for a special treat!" added Angel Cake.

And that's exactly what we did!

Special
Treats

Blueberry Muffin's
Snowman Sundaes

Make a frosty snowman right in your kitchen—
with ice cream! These sundaes are lots of fun
to make with your friends.

INGREDIENTS

For each snowman sundae, you will need:

3 scoops vanilla ice cream

4 chocolate-covered pretzel sticks

1 chocolate marshmallow

1 chocolate wafer cookie

Assorted small candies for decorating
(you can use peppermints, gumdrops,
miniature chocolate candies, jelly beans,
candy buttons, sprinkles, miniature
marshmallows, or any other small candies
you have)

SUPPLIES

Glass serving bowl
Spoon

TIP

If you don't
have chocolate marshmallows
and chocolate wafer cookies, you
can still make a hat for your snowman out of vanilla marshmallows
and cookies. It will look great
and taste great, too!

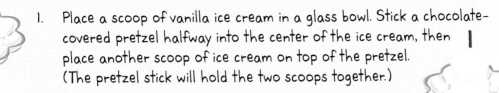

1. Place a scoop of vanilla ice cream in a glass bowl. Stick a chocolate-covered pretzel halfway into the center of the ice cream, then place another scoop of ice cream on top of the pretzel. (The pretzel stick will hold the two scoops together.)

2. Place another pretzel stick into the second scoop of ice cream, then top with a third scoop of ice cream. You made a snowman!

3. To make the snowman's arms, insert two chocolate-covered pretzel sticks on either side of the second scoop of ice cream.

4. To make a hat for the snowman, place the chocolate wafer cookie on top of the snowman's head for the brim, then top with a chocolate marshmallow.

5. Use the assorted small candies to decorate the snowman however you want. You can give him a friendly face and a row of colorful buttons, or tie a licorice rope around his neck for a scarf. Have fun!

Ginger Snap's
Gingerbread House

A gingerbread house takes a lot of time to make—but it's worth it! Make sure you have at least two or three days to make the house.

INGREDIENTS

1 cup butter, softened

2 cups brown sugar

1 cup white sugar

$\frac{1}{4}$ cup molasses

3 eggs

$6\frac{1}{2}$ cups flour

2 teaspoons baking soda

$\frac{1}{4}$ teaspoon salt

$\frac{1}{2}$ tablespoon ginger

1 tablespoon cinnamon

$\frac{1}{2}$ tablespoon nutmeg

5–6 batches of Royal Icing (see recipe on page 69—make up the icing only as you need it)

Assorted small candies for decorating (you can use peppermints, gumdrops, miniature chocolate candies, jelly beans, candy buttons, sprinkles, miniature marshmallows, or any other small candies you have)

SUPPLIES

Ruler, pencil, and waxed paper

12 x 12-inch piece of clean cardboard

Foil

Tape

Baking trays

Paper towel

2 bowls (medium and large)

Measuring cups and spoons

Electric mixer

Sifter

Wooden spoon

Rolling pin

Dish towel

Knife

Spatula

Pastry bag

Canned goods (to be used as supports)

Butter knife

TIP

Only make the Royal Icing as you need it, otherwise it will dry out and be hard to use.

DAY 1: <u>MIX</u> AND <u>BAKE</u> THE HOUSE.

1. Before you begin any baking, you will need to make a template for the house. Use the ruler, pencil, and waxed paper to draw the pattern for the house, then cut the pieces out. You will need four pattern pieces, one for the front and back, one for the gables, one for the sides, and one for the roof.

   Front and Back (square): 6 x 6 inches   Gables (triangle): 6 x 3 $\frac{3}{4}$ x 3 $\frac{3}{4}$ inches

   Sides (rectangle): 7 x 6 inches   Roof (rectangle): 7 x 5 $\frac{1}{2}$ inches

   After you have cut out the front and back and the gable patterns, tape the square and triangle together so that they make one pattern piece.

2. Next, make the base for the house. Cover the piece of cardboard with foil and securely tape the edges of the foil beneath the base.

 3. <u>Preheat</u> the oven to 350 degrees.

4. Line some baking trays with foil, then use the paper towel to rub the foil with a small amount of vegetable oil. Sprinkle the foil with a small amount of flour.

 5. Now <u>mix</u> the dough. In the large bowl, <u>cream</u> together the butter, white sugar, brown sugar, and molasses using the electric mixer. Add the eggs and <u>beat</u> until fluffy.

6. In the medium bowl, <u>sift</u> together the flour, baking soda, salt, ginger, cinnamon, and nutmeg.

7. Add the dry ingredients to the wet ingredients. Stir until just combined. Then <u>knead</u> the dough with your hands until it is smooth.

8. Sprinkle some flour on a clean, dry surface, and roll out $\frac{1}{4}$ of the dough until it's $\frac{1}{4}$ inch thick. Cover the rest of the dough in the bowl with a dish towel to keep it from drying out.

 9. Place one of the pattern pieces on top of the dough and use the sharp knife to cut around it. You will need to make one front, one back, two sides, and two roof pieces. If you want, use the sharp knife to cut doors and windows out of the front, back, and sides of the house.

10. As you need more, roll out another $\frac{1}{4}$ of the dough, keeping the rest of the dough covered with the dish towel to keep it from drying out. Repeat step 9 until all the pieces of the house have been cut out.

 11. Use the spatula to carefully transfer the pieces of dough to the baking trays.

12. <u>Bake</u> the dough for 10–20 minutes, or until firm. Let the pieces of the house cool on the trays overnight. They won't taste as fresh if you decide to eat the house, but it will be a lot easier to build with them.

DAY 2: BUILD THE HOUSE.

1. First, make 2-3 batches of Royal Icing according to the recipe on the next page.

2. Fill a pastry bag with icing, and pipe two lines of icing on the base. The icing lines should look like an L—a shorter line, 4 inches long, for one side; and a longer line, 8 inches long, for the front.

3. For this step, you'll need an extra pair of hands! Carefully balance the front wall and a side wall on the icing lines. While holding the pieces in place, pipe more icing in the joint between the two walls to cement them together. Hold the walls together until the icing is set, about 15-20 minutes. You can use some clean cans to prop up the walls to make it easier.

4. Next, pipe another 4-inch line of icing for the other side wall. Stand the wall on the line of icing and add more icing between the front and the back. Hold the side wall to the front wall until the icing is set.

5. Finally, pipe an 8-inch line of icing for the back wall. Balance the last wall on the base and pipe more icing on either side of the wall to cement it to the two side walls. Hold the walls in place until they are set, then let the house sit for an hour so that all the icing is dry.

6. Now it's time to add the roof! This is the most challenging part of all, so be patient and work slowly. Pipe lots of icing around all the edges of the house. Carefully add the two roof pieces, one at a time, making sure they touch at the top and equally overhang the sides. Add more icing to the hinge of the roof and hold the roof in place until the icing is dry (balancing the roof on some clean cans is the easiest way to do this).

7. It's best to let the house sit quietly overnight to make sure that all of the icing is solidly dry. In the meantime, you can get all of the yummy candy toppings ready!

DAY 3: DECORATE THE HOUSE.

1. Make another 2 batches of Royal Icing according to the recipe below.

2. Evenly spread icing across both sides of the roof. Decorate the roof with candy.

3. Fill the pastry bag with icing and use it to draw the outlines of windows and doors on the house (if you didn't cut them out before the house was baked).

4. Use icing as glue to attach more candies to the house. You can decorate your gingerbread house however you want. Have fun!

Royal Icing

INGREDIENTS
3 egg whites
1 teaspoon cream of tartar
3 cups powdered sugar

SUPPLIES
Medium bowl
Measuring cups and spoons
Electric mixer
Spatula

TIP

Separating eggs can be a little tricky, but once you've done it a few times, it will be berry easy! Gently tap the egg on a bowl so that the shell cracks around the middle of the egg. Carefully open the egg with the large end down (the yolk will stay in the large end). Holding the egg over a bowl, transfer the yolk back and forth between each half of the shell. The egg white will spill out of the shell into the bowl, leaving the yolk behind.

1. Put all of the ingredients into the bowl.

2. <u>Beat</u> the ingredients together with an electric mixer for 5 minutes until the icing is smooth and shiny.

Huckleberry Pie's
Mini Candy House

These miniature candy houses are berry easy to make, and lots of fun, too! Make a whole bunch of them for a cute (and yummy!) little village.

INGREDIENTS
- Graham crackers (you will need 7 for each house)
- 1 batch of Royal Icing (see recipe on page 69)
- Assorted small candies for decorating (you can use peppermints, gumdrops, miniature chocolate candies, jelly beans, candy buttons, sprinkles, miniature marshmallows, or any other small candies you have)

SUPPLIES
- Small plate (one for each house)
- Pastry bag
- Butter knife

1. Place one graham cracker flat on the plate (this is the base of the house). Use the pastry bag to pipe a thin line of icing along each edge of the graham cracker.

 2. Use two more graham crackers to make two of the walls. Stand each graham cracker on an adjoining line of icing and pipe another line of icing along the corner where the two walls join.

 3. Repeat step 2 to make the other two walls. Let the house sit for 15–20 minutes, or until the icing has hardened and the walls are stable.

 4. Now use the last two graham crackers to make the roof. Pipe a line of icing along opposite walls of the house. Carefully balance the graham crackers on the icing so that they make a triangle. The top edges of the graham crackers will touch. Use more icing to secure the top of the roof and let the house sit until the icing has hardened and the roof is secure.

5. Use the butter knife to carefully spread a layer of icing on the flat sides of the roof. It will look like the roof is covered in snow. If the icing drips off the edges of the roof a bit, it's okay—it will look like icicles.

6. Decorate the house by using extra icing to pipe the outlines of windows and doors. Then add candy decorations, using more icing as glue to hold them in place.

TIP

Don't forget to decorate around the house, too. You can make a path to the house out of chocolate candies, bushes out of gumdrops, or a fence out of chocolate-covered pretzels.

Special Treats

Strawberry Shortcake's
Strawberry-Jelly Donuts

These special donuts have a special name—
sufganiyot. They are delicious treats for Hanukkah!

INGREDIENTS

- ¾ cup milk
- 1 package dry yeast
- ½ cup white sugar
- 2½ cups flour
- <u>Pinch</u> of salt
- 2 eggs
- ½ teaspoon cinnamon
- 2 tablespoons butter, softened
- ½ cup strawberry jelly
- Vegetable oil for frying
- Powdered sugar for dusting

SUPPLIES

- Small microwave-safe bowl
- Measuring cups and spoons
- Wooden spoon
- Sifter
- 2 bowls (medium and large)
- Electric mixer
- Dish towel
- Rolling pin
- Round cookie cutter
- Frying pan
- Plate
- Paper towel
- Tongs

1. Warm the milk in the microwave (it should be slightly warm, not hot). Dissolve the yeast and 2 tablespoons of white sugar in the milk, stirring a few times with the wooden spoon. Set aside for 10 minutes.

2. <u>Sift</u> the flour and salt into the large bowl, then make a well in the center of the flour and pour in the yeast mixture. <u>Stir</u> the dough together with the wooden spoon until it is well combined.

  3. In the medium bowl, <u>beat</u> together the eggs, the cinnamon, and the rest of the white sugar.

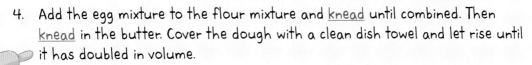 4. Add the egg mixture to the flour mixture and <u>knead</u> until combined. Then <u>knead</u> in the butter. Cover the dough with a clean dish towel and let rise until it has doubled in volume.

5. Sprinkle some flour on a clean, dry surface and <u>roll</u> out the dough to $\frac{1}{4}$ inch thick. Use the cookie cutter to cut circles of dough, then <u>roll</u> each circle of dough into a ball.

6. Use your finger to make an indentation in each ball of dough. Fill the indentation with $\frac{1}{2}$ to 1 teaspoon of strawberry jelly, then push the dough back over the jam so that the jam is completely enclosed in the donut.

7. Line the plate with paper towels.

 8. Heat 2 inches of vegetable oil in a frying pan. Gently place the donuts in the pan and <u>fry</u> until golden brown on both sides, turning several times with the tongs. Carefully remove the donuts from the oil and let cool on paper towels.

 9. While the donuts are still warm, <u>sift</u> powdered sugar on top of them.

TIP

Always have an adult <u>fry</u> food in hot oil, and be careful—it can easily splatter or splash.

Angel Cake's
Meringue Kisses

These sweet treats are like puffy little clouds! They taste great by themselves or with a little chocolate surprise hidden inside. Make them extra special with a drizzle of strawberry sauce. Yum!

INGREDIENTS

- 2 egg whites
- 1 teaspoon vanilla
- $\frac{1}{4}$ teaspoon salt
- $\frac{3}{4}$ cup white sugar
- 1 cup miniature chocolate chips (optional)

SUPPLIES

- Baking tray
- Foil
- Medium bowl
- Measuring cups and spoons
- Electric mixer
- Spatula
- Wire rack

1. <u>Preheat</u> the oven to 225 degrees.

2. Line a baking tray with foil.

 3. In the medium bowl, measure the vanilla and salt. Add the egg whites and <u>beat</u> with the electric mixer until stiff peaks form.

 4. Slowly sprinkle the sugar over the egg white mixture, and keep mixing until the batter is stiff and shiny.

 5. Add the chocolate chips (if you're using them) and gently fold them into the egg whites with a spatula.

 6. Drop teaspoons of batter onto the baking tray and <u>bake</u> for 2 hours or until the meringues are very pale yellow on the bottom (the rest of the meringues will be white). When the meringues are done, they will peel easily off the baking tray; if they stick, let them <u>bake</u> longer. Carefully transfer the meringues to a wire rack to cool.

7. If you want, make a batch of strawberry glaze according to the recipe on page 56. Just before serving, drizzle the strawberry sauce over the meringue kisses.

TIP

It's best to make meringues on a dry day—if the weather is too humid or wet, they will take a really long time to dry out in the oven.

Candy House Village

It was the middle of December and the holidays were right around the corner! I wanted to make some berry special presents for my friends, but I just couldn't figure out what.

"Let's see . . ." I said to Apple Dumplin'. "The presents have to be berry special. They have to be as different as my friends and as wonderful as they are, too! Do you have any ideas, sweetie?"

But Apple just smiled as she sucked on a candy cane from a bowl full of Christmas candy.

"Christmas candy!" I exclaimed. "I can make a miniature candy house for each one of my friends—and I can decorate them so that they look just like my friends' houses! Then we can invite all of our friends over and they will be berry surprised by their presents."

I started working on the little candy houses right away. Apple helped me make a batch of Royal Icing, and then we carefully made six little houses—one for Angel Cake, one for Orange Blossom, one for Blueberry Muffin, one for Ginger Snap, and one for Huckleberry Pie. We even made one to keep for ourselves!

"Now comes the fun part, Apple," I said. "It's time to decorate the houses!" We made Huck's candy house look just like his fort by putting chocolate-colored pretzels all over it. For Blueberry Muffin's house we attached little blue

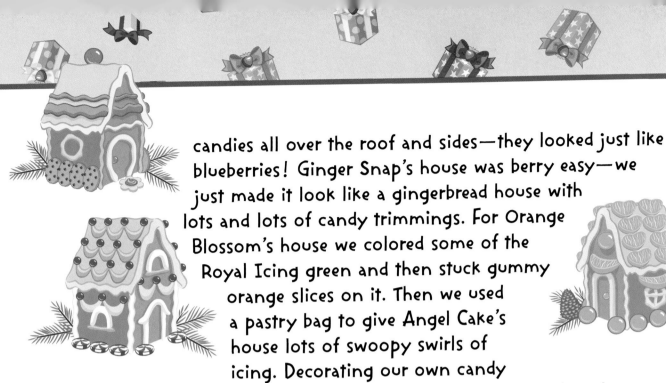

candies all over the roof and sides—they looked just like blueberries! Ginger Snap's house was berry easy—we just made it look like a gingerbread house with lots and lots of candy trimmings. For Orange Blossom's house we colored some of the Royal Icing green and then stuck gummy orange slices on it. Then we used a pastry bag to give Angel Cake's house lots of swoopy swirls of icing. Decorating our own candy house was berry easy—we covered it in red icing and put tiny chocolate chips all over it to look like strawberry seeds!

The next day, I invited all my friends over to play. They were berry excited to see their candy houses! Blueberry Muffin even took a picture of them all together.

"Of course everybody wants to take his or her house home," she explained. "But I don't want to forget how special the houses look all together!"

And that was the berry nicest thing anyone could have said!

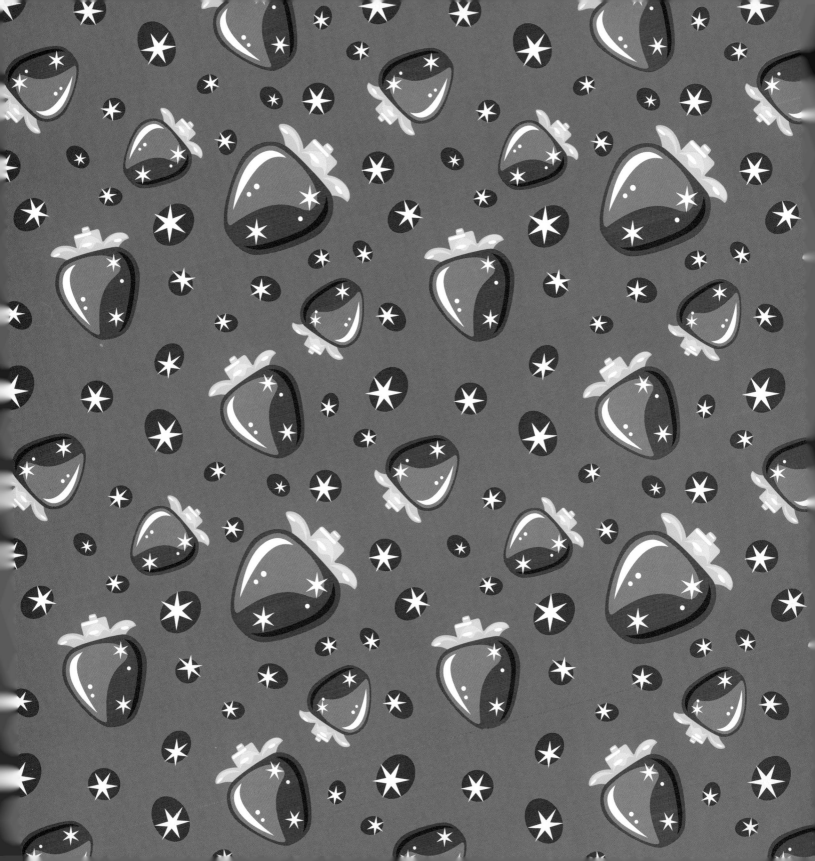

Snacks & Drinks

Orange Blossom's
Reindeer Snacks

It's berry nice to leave a snack for hungry reindeer on Christmas Eve! They love fresh vegetables— and while you're at it, why not make some for yourself?

INGREDIENTS

- 1 red pepper
- 1 green pepper
- 1 cucumber
- 1 pint cherry tomatoes
- ½ package of baby carrots
- ½ bunch of celery

For the dip:
- 2 cups sour cream
- 1 packet onion soup mix or 1 packet ranch dressing mix

SUPPLIES

- Measuring cups
- Small bowl
- Whisk
- Cutting board and knife
- Serving platter or plate

TIP

Always wash fresh vegetables before you eat them— even the pre-washed ones, like the baby carrots.

1. First, make the dip. Measure the sour cream into the small bowl; <u>whisk</u> the onion soup mix or ranch dressing mix into the sour cream until fully blended. Refrigerate for at least 30 minutes to let the flavors mix.

2. While the dip is chilling, wash all of the vegetables.

3. Cut the red and green peppers into 2-inch sticks. <u>Slice</u> the cucumber into rounds. Trim the ends of the celery and cut each stalk into 2-inch sticks.

4. Arrange the red and green pepper slices, the cucumber rounds, the carrots, the tomatoes, and the celery sticks on a plate. Place the bowl of dip in the center. Have fun snacking!

Huckleberry Pie's
Cheese Coins

These cheesy snack crackers look like Hanukkah coins called *gelt*. They're easy to make and delicious, too!

TIP
To save time, you can buy cheese that's already been grated.

INGREDIENTS
1 stick butter, chilled and cut into 1-inch pieces
1½ cups grated cheddar cheese
1 cup flour
¼ teaspoon salt (use ⅛ teaspoon if the butter is salted)

SUPPLIES
Measuring cups and spoons
Food processor
Plastic wrap and foil
Rolling pin
Baking tray
Cutting board and knife
Spatula
Wire rack

1. In the food processor, pulse together the butter, cheese, flour, and salt until the mixture forms clumps the size of small peas. If you don't have a food processor, you can use a pastry blender to do this by hand— it will just take a little longer.

2. Use your hands to form the dough into a ball. Wrap it in plastic wrap and refrigerate for an hour.

3. Preheat the oven to 400 degrees.

4. Separate the dough into three equal pieces. Roll each piece of dough into a log shape about 1 inch wide. If the dough still feels thoroughly chilled, continue with the next step. If not, wrap each log in plastic wrap and refrigerate for another hour.

5. Line a baking tray with foil.

6. Slice each log into thin, ¼-inch-thick slices.

7. Place the slices on the baking tray and bake for 10–12 minutes, or until golden. Use the spatula to carefully transfer the crackers to a wire rack to cool.

Snacks & Drinks

Angel Cake's
Latkes

These yummy fried potato pancakes are great for a snack or a side dish.

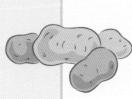

INGREDIENTS
4 potatoes
1 onion
2 eggs
1 teaspoon salt
3 tablespoons flour
Vegetable oil for frying

SUPPLIES
Peeler
Grater
Cutting board and knife
2 bowls (small and large)
Whisk
Wooden spoon
Measuring spoons
Plate or baking tray
Paper towel
Frying pan
Spatula

1. Wash and <u>peel</u> the potatoes, then <u>grate</u> them. <u>Chop</u> the onion.

2. <u>Stir</u> together the grated potatoes and onion in the large bowl.

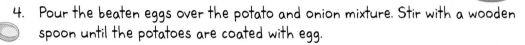

3. In the small bowl, <u>beat</u> the eggs and the salt.

4. Pour the beaten eggs over the potato and onion mixture. Stir with a wooden spoon until the potatoes are coated with egg.

5. Sprinkle the flour evenly over the potatoes and <u>stir</u> well.

6. Line a large plate or baking tray with paper towels.

 7. Heat about an inch of oil in the frying pan. For each latke, carefully drop 2 tablespoons of the potato mixture into the oil.

 8. Use the back of a spatula to flatten the latkes so they are evenly shaped. <u>Fry</u> each side for about 5 minutes over medium heat, or until golden-brown.

 9. Carefully remove the latkes from the frying pan and <u>drain</u> on the paper towels. Serve hot with sour cream or applesauce (try the applesauce recipe on the next page).

TIP

<u>Mix</u> in grated sweet potatoes or beets for some brightly colored latkes—yum!

Apple Dumplin's
Easy Applesauce

Once you see how easy it is to make homemade applesauce, you'll want to make it all the time! It's one of my baby sister's favorite snacks.

INGREDIENTS

4 apples
½ cup water
¼–½ cup sugar (to taste)

SUPPLIES

Peeler
Cutting board and knife
Medium-sized pot
Measuring cups and spoons

1. Wash, peel, and core the apples. Chop them into tiny, evenly sized pieces.

2. Put the apples into the pot and cover with water. Bring to a boil, reduce the heat, and simmer for 10 minutes.

3. Stir in the sugar to taste and simmer for another 5–10 minutes, or until apples are very soft.

4. Carefully drain the apples in the colander and pour them into the food processor or blender. Purée until the applesauce is smooth.

TIP

If you like cinnamon, add ¼ teaspoon to the apples as they cook. Yum!

Blueberry Muffin's
Cranberry Sauce

This homemade cranberry sauce is tart and tangy, with lots of good flavors. All of my friends love it!

INGREDIENTS
2 cups fresh cranberries
1 cup water
1 cup brown sugar

SUPPLIES
Colander
Measuring cups and spoons
Medium-sized pot
Wooden spoon
Glass bowl

TIP
This recipe is berry simple, but you can make it fancier by adding one or more of the following ingredients:
$\frac{1}{2}$ cup orange juice
$\frac{1}{2}$ of a chopped apple
$\frac{1}{4}$ cup raisins
$\frac{1}{2}$ teaspoon cinnamon

1. Wash and <u>drain</u> the cranberries using a colander.

 2. Put the cranberries, water, and brown sugar in the pot, and bring to a <u>boil</u> over medium heat. Cook the cranberries until the sauce is thick, <u>stirring</u> constantly with a wooden spoon.

 3. Carefully pour the cranberry sauce into a glass bowl and allow to cool.

4. When the bowl is slightly warm to the touch, refrigerate the cranberry sauce. Serve cold.

Strawberry Shortcake's
Trim the Tree Mini-Pizzas

These mini-pizzas are berry fun to make!

INGREDIENTS

6 bagels or English muffins,
    split in half
12 tablespoons pizza sauce
    or spaghetti sauce
3 cups shredded mozzarella cheese
1 green pepper
Any other toppings you'd like: red
    pepper, yellow pepper, black
    olives, mushrooms, or pepperoni

SUPPLIES

Baking tray
Foil
Measuring cups and spoons
Cutting board and knife
Spoon

TIP

You can use the toppings to make other shapes on your pizzas, too— like a star or a smiley face. Have fun!

  1. <u>Preheat</u> the oven to 350 degrees.

2. Line the baking tray with foil.

3. Wash all of the vegetables.

  4. Cut the green pepper into 1½-inch-long sticks. The green pepper sticks will be the branches of your tree.

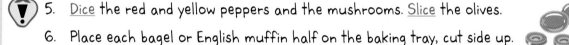 5. <u>Dice</u> the red and yellow peppers and the mushrooms. <u>Slice</u> the olives.

6. Place each bagel or English muffin half on the baking tray, cut side up.

7. Spread 2 tablespoons of sauce on each pizza. Then sprinkle ½ cup shredded cheese over the sauce on each pizza.

8. Arrange the green pepper sticks so that they look like the branches of a pine tree. Then use the rest of the toppings to "decorate" your tree! You could use the yellow pepper to make a star at the top of the tree, and use the red pepper pieces and olive slices to make ornaments.

9. <u>Bake</u> the pizzas in the oven for 10–12 minutes, or until the cheese is golden and bubbly.

Angel Cake's
Snowman Buns

These yummy buns look like funny little snowmen!
They taste just a little sweet, with a nice vanilla flavor.

INGREDIENTS

For the buns:
- 1 packet of dry yeast
- $\frac{1}{2}$ cup warm water
- $\frac{1}{3}$ cup white sugar
- 1 teaspoon salt
- $\frac{1}{4}$ cup butter, melted
- 1 egg
- $\frac{3}{4}$ cup milk
- 1 teaspoon vanilla
- 1 cup flour
- 1 cup raisins

For the glaze:
- 1 egg, beaten
- $\frac{1}{2}$ cup white sugar

SUPPLIES

- 2 bowls (small and large)
- Measuring cups and spoons
- Wooden spoon
- Electric mixer
- Dish towel
- Baking tray
- Foil
- Brush
- Spatula
- Wire rack

TIP

Make sure the water you use in step 1 is warm, not hot—hot water will kill the yeast and keep the buns from rising. If the yeast isn't foamy after 5 minutes, throw it out and try again with a new packet.

1. Dissolve the yeast in the warm water in the small bowl, and set aside. After 5 minutes, the yeast should be frothy and foamy.

 2. <u>Combine</u> the white sugar, salt, melted butter, egg, milk, and vanilla in the large bowl and <u>beat</u> with an electric mixer until the ingredients are combined. <u>Mix</u> in the yeast and flour until the dough clumps together.

3. Cover the bowl with a dish towel and let sit in a warm place for an hour, or until it has doubled in size.

4. Place the dough on a lightly floured surface and <u>knead</u> it with your hands a few times so that it is smooth and uniform.

5. Line a baking tray with foil.

6. Now it's time to make the snowmen! You will need five balls of dough for each snowman: three for the body and two smaller ones for the arms. The head ball should be about 1 inch in diameter, the middle ball should be $1\frac{1}{2}$ inches in diameter, and the bottom ball should be 2 inches in diameter. The arm balls should each be $\frac{1}{2}$ inch in diameter.

7. Arrange the five balls on the tray to make a snowman shape, making sure that they are all touching. When the snowmen are formed, cover them with a dish towel and let them rise again for another hour.

 8. <u>Preheat</u> the oven to 350 degrees.

9. Give each snowman a face and buttons with the raisins. Brush the snowmen with the beaten egg, then sprinkle with white sugar.

 10. <u>Bake</u> the snowmen for 15–18 minutes, or until golden brown. Use the spatula to carefully transfer them to the wire rack.

Ginger Snap's
Cinnamon Popovers

Popovers are like big, puffy muffins!
I like to eat mine with strawberry jam.

INGREDIENTS
$\frac{1}{4}$ cup white sugar
1 teaspoon cinnamon
1 cup flour
$\frac{1}{4}$ teaspoon salt
2 eggs
1 cup milk
1 tablespoon butter, melted

SUPPLIES
Muffin tray or popover pan
3 bowls (small, medium, and large)
Measuring cups and spoons
Wooden spoon

TIP

It's berry important not to overbeat the popover batter—if you do, the popovers won't be big and fluffy.

1. <u>Preheat</u> the oven to 425 degrees.

2. <u>Grease</u> and flour a muffin tray or popover pan.

3. In the small bowl, <u>stir</u> together the sugar and cinnamon; set aside.

4. <u>Stir</u> together the flour and salt in the medium bowl; set aside.

5. In the large bowl, <u>whisk</u> together the eggs and the milk until blended.

6. Add the flour mixture to the egg mixture and <u>stir</u> with a wooden spoon just until the ingredients are combined. The batter should have some bubbles in it.

7. Pour the batter into the prepared pan, filling each cup $\frac{2}{3}$ of the way full. Sprinkle the cinnamon sugar over the top of each popover.

8. <u>Bake</u> for 30 minutes, then reduce the heat to 350 degrees and <u>bake</u> for an additional 15–20 minutes, or until the popovers have doubled in size and are deep golden brown. Serve warm, with butter and jam.

Huckleberry Pie's
Hot Cocoa

This warm, chocolatey cocoa is the perfect drink on a cold winter's day.

INGREDIENTS

4 cups milk
8 tablespoons cocoa powder
1 cup sugar

SUPPLIES

Small bowl
Measuring cups and spoons

Small pot
Wooden spoon

 1. In a small bowl, <u>mix</u> together the cocoa powder and the sugar.

 2. Warm the milk in the pot over medium heat.

 3. Add the cocoa and sugar mixture one tablespoon at a time, stirring until the cocoa has just the right amount of chocolate for you.

TIP
Make your hot chocolate extra special by adding marshmallows or whipped cream and chocolate shavings.

Blueberry Muffin's
Peppermint Hot Chocolate

Warm chocolate milk with a little bit of peppermint is a berry special holiday drink! Blueberry Muffin makes the best peppermint hot chocolate ever.

INGREDIENTS

4 cups milk
4 ounces semisweet chocolate, chopped

$\frac{1}{3}$ cup white sugar
$\frac{1}{4}$ teaspoon peppermint extract

SUPPLIES

Measuring cups and spoons
Small pot
Wooden spoon

 1. <u>Combine</u> the milk, sugar, and chocolate in a small pot over low heat. <u>Stir</u> constantly with a wooden spoon until the chocolate and sugar are melted and all ingredients are combined.

2. <u>Stir</u> in the peppermint extract and serve.

TIP
Add a candy cane to each mug of hot chocolate for even more peppermint flavor.

Angel Cake's
Vanilla Milk

I like to drink a warm mug of vanilla milk before I go to bed. It's berry yummy!

INGREDIENTS

4 cups milk
4 tablespoons sugar
1 teaspoon vanilla extract

SUPPLIES
Measuring cups and spoons
Small pot
Wooden spoon

TIP
Add some whipped cream (see the recipe on page 45) to your vanilla milk for a treat.

1. <u>Combine</u> the milk, sugar, and vanilla in a small pot.
2. <u>Stir</u> constantly over low heat until the sugar is dissolved.

Ginger Snap's
Sweetly Spiced Nog

This drink is usually called "egg nog," but Ginger Snap leaves out the eggs because it's not safe to drink raw eggs.

INGREDIENTS
$3\frac{1}{2}$ cups milk
$\frac{1}{2}$ cup cream
$\frac{1}{2}$ teaspoon vanilla

$\frac{1}{8}$ teaspoon nutmeg
$\frac{1}{8}$ teaspoon cinnamon
$\frac{1}{4}$ cup sugar

SUPPLIES
Large bowl
Measuring cups and spoons
Whisk
Pitcher

TIP

Traditional egg nog only has nutmeg, not cinnamon, so if you want to leave out the cinnamon, just make sure you use $\frac{1}{4}$ teaspoon nutmeg.

1. <u>Combine</u> all ingredients in a large bowl, and <u>whisk</u> until they are well-blended and the sugar is dissolved.

2. Pour the nog into a pitcher and refrigerate until thoroughly chilled.

Apple Dumplin's
Spiced Apple Cider

Hot apple cider with yummy spices is a wonderful fall and winter treat! Apple Dumplin' and I always make some after we go apple picking.

INGREDIENTS

4 cups apple juice
6 cinnamon sticks
1 teaspoon cloves

SUPPLIES

Measuring cups and spoons
Small pot
Wooden spoon
Colander
Pitcher

TIP

Try fresh-squeezed apple juice or apple cider.

1. <u>Combine</u> all ingredients in a small pot and simmer on low for 15 minutes.

2. Use the colander to <u>drain</u> the cider into a large bowl or pitcher. Throw out the cinnamon sticks and cloves.

3. Serve each mug of hot apple cider with a fresh cinnamon stick as a stirrer.

Holiday Fruit Punch

This yummy punch is delicious to serve at holiday parties.

INGREDIENTS

2 cups cranberry juice
2 cups grape juice
4 cups apple juice

SUPPLIES

Measuring cups
Punch bowl

1. Stir together all of the ingredients in the punch bowl. Chill until ready to serve.

TIP

If you are going to serve this punch at a party, freeze some of it in ice cube trays. When you serve it, add the punch ice cubes to the bowl. They will keep the punch nice and cold without watering it down as they melt.

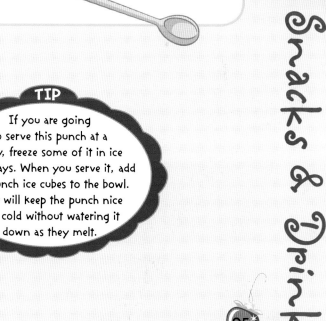

Index